EMERGING

FROM THE

ROCK

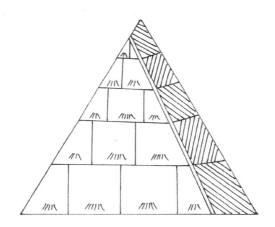

Printed in the United States of America by BookLogix

ISBN 978-1-7338408-0-4

Cover and Text Design by Rebecca Shaw; BrockleyDesigns.com

Cover illustration by Joan Shirkey Walters

Illustration on page 53 by Sam Pillsbury

This book can be purchased from Amazon.com

All profits from the sale of this book will be donated to charity.

For comments and feedback please email Joan at:
joanswalters@gmail.com

EMERGING

FROM THE

ROCK

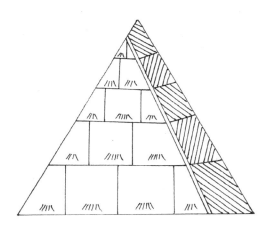

JOAN SHIRKEY WALTERS

Dedication

For Mike, who is of the Earth

Table of Contents

Take these words
Make them yours
Or let them evoke
Your own truth
For that is their purpose
To clarify the obscure
To splice the broken
To transcend time
To illumine new truths
On my path
On your path
On our paths together.

Touch the Earth
Let it ground your pain
So that you become as strong as the rock.

Feel the Rain
Let it wash your fears into the rivers
To be at peace in the sea.

Feel the sacred Wind
Purifying you with truth
Bringing knowledge to your heart.

Be the Fire
Let it burn your anger
Transforming it into love
As the sacred smoke
Rises to the Source.

Feeling the wall
Cool nooks
And crannies
The rough surface
Of crafted rock
Speaking to me
Of my anger
And my fear
I asked:

        "Why do you
         Stand before me
        Blocking my path
        Sending me into
        Turmoil
        Confusion
         Immobility?"

"I love you
For you are
Part of me
But can you provide
Steps toward my
Dreams
Instead of an
Impasse?"

The spiral broken
Perfection lost
With curves
Spinning off
At odd angles
Curiously askew
Remembering
Something
Which called them
Into moving circles
Revolving
Perfectly
In measured
Space
An ordered
Whole.

Earth is our home
Our bodies
Provide us with physical form
But we are also spirit
Intertwined
Sometimes in balance
Sometimes not
Feeling pulled to one side
Or turned inside out
These struggles bring pain
But there are things
We can do here
Which cannot be done
Elsewhere
So our choices
Matter greatly
What is done
And what is not.

Rocks
Split asunder
Projectiles waiting
To be sent into space
Whales, dolphins beckoning
From peaceful depths
Great arks
Holding covenants
Sacred as life's breath
Instructed in
Ancient ways
They rest
Without constraint
Emitting protection
They evoke
Timelessness, strength
Infused with power
They hold
Spiraling
Energy
Entranced
Entrained.

Rock-strewn giant
Heart upthrown
Offering all
Amidst standing walls
And jagged crevices
Surely ancient voices
Sing here
Songs of wisdom
Dreaming deep.

Little winged
Darting one
You remind me
Of some jerky
Maneuvering
In my life
But I have
No wings
To lift me
On my rounds
Only feet
Firmly planted
On the ground.

The Spirit Ones
Imprinted on my soul
There, forever, for me to know
Voices singing

Ancient beeches
Spaces ringing
With life long gone
But never lost
The forest holds
These energies
In the quiet
In the wind
And my calling

Touches them
They respond
Not palpably
But in the sound
Their answers
Fill me with longing
For lives unknown

For a way at one
Not undone.

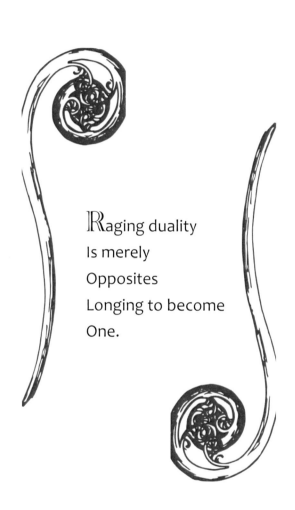

Raging duality
Is merely
Opposites
Longing to become
One.

There are things
That we choose
To bring
Into this world
Just as there are things
We release
Which never materialize
And we must live
With our choices
Knowing that we cannot
Do it all

We may feel peace
With our pursuits
Or we may be haunted
By things
Unformed, unborn
The struggle is
To come to terms
With possibilities
Both realized
And not.

I am standing
On a mountain top
Gazing down ridges
Tumbling
One on another
Moving in mist
To infinity

Another vista is
Valleys
The level ground between
Nourished by giants
Gentle, serene

I am coming
To some uncertain
Precarious path
Choosing
One course
Over another
Only because
Sunset is falling

And as light flares
Spectacular
Washing the sky
Night drops over
Mountain tops
Quietly enveloping
Ridges and valleys

The day is gone
And I must move on.

I tried to impart
Some of my heart
You listened
As though preoccupied
Not acknowledging
Not even a smile
 I felt the words
Were not reaching you
Because when there is
Understanding
 A flow of energy
Moves beyond words
A harmonic sounds
Two notes are linked
Resonating
Making each
More than it was
Before.

Our prayers for rain
Were like adding
One drop of water
To the storm's intent
In favor of moisture
Being loosened
On the Earth
So our wishes
Mattered
They were not unheeded
And yet
The storm might
Just as easily
Have chosen
To save that drop
For another day
Blowing itself
To another place
So we give thanks.

The patterns that are woven
Into our lives
Provide form to our experience
Substance to our actions
But so often we do not see
Their points of origin
Their destinations
Sometimes we even
Close our eyes to them
Resisting the knowledge
Of the divine design
Fleeing from connections
Because we are afraid
To listen to our deepest desires
We choose to grasp fragments instead
Their sharp edges
Cutting our hands and psyches
Preventing us from
Doing the work we are called to do
Sapping us of purpose
Depleting the richness of our lives.

Tragedy, pain
Evoke contact with sources
We would not otherwise engage.

The fire
Lifted each page
Enveloping it
In flames
Edging the evil
With brightness
Just as they
Could choose
Darkness
Or light
And as it burned
Monstrous shapes
Rose, curled and fell
Like the destruction
They had wrought
On each other
And their children
Poisoned
Imprisoned in hate
With no desire
To escape
Only wishing to kill
Blackened and burned
Like each page
Leaving only empty shells
Of lives
Brittle and betrayed.

The sharp corners
Of my finiteness
Hitting me
At every turn
Anger, frustration
Limited energy
I cannot do anything
Today

My depths
Go untouched
My heights are neglected
No soaring
Earthbound
Drained
No more to give

So don't ask me
For anything
Until tomorrow
Then perhaps
My well
Will be filled
My cell
Opened

But now I am
Empty
Confined
Crackling and dry
Bound
No water
No fire.

The shadows can be
As lovely
As the light
Because
Nightfall is
As much
Of the cycle
As the dawn
Not all can stand
The full unveiling
Of sun
Some
Benefit
From the
Shelter of darkness
Until they have
Prepared themselves.

What to say
When words only seem
To play
With feelings
Deep
Or experiences
Barely grasped
In other planes

When does the truth
Demand
Its own response
When does it need to
Blossom
Unbid
Within the heart
And not come
From without

So stand in love
Transmit strength
And gently offer
Words
Which may
Awaken
Beauty
And
Grace.

Being close to death is like
The last long rays of light
Striking the trees' uppermost branches
At sunset.

Now that your life is ending
What needs to be conveyed
Spoken and unspoken
To free the hearts
Of those you leave behind
How do you assess
Things done and undone
What perspective can you find
To soften regrets
To forgive harm
To gain new insight into pain
So that your soul is freed
To rise above this plane
Cleansed of the old
Welcoming truth
Then death dances proudly
And you are renewed.

There is no separation
Between loss and pain
They are the same.

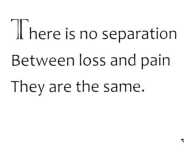

I want to release my pain
For I have other things
To carry in my heart.

There are
Eternal
Universal
Patterns
That are required
Of us all
And we each
Stand in different places
We find
Different distances
In relation
To rock
And spirit
But as energy Is always in flux
We are all
Eventually
Required to choose
To cling to the rock
Or to emerge from it.

Just as the various
Creatures
Plants
Elements
In the forest
Transform energy
Into usable forms
For each other
So too can we humans
Create
Opportunities
Structures
Processes
For each other's
Growth
Making energy
Available for
That purpose.

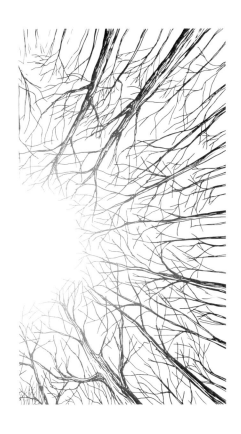

Give freely
As it is given to you
For you are
Not the beginning
Or the end
Rather
The interval
The span between
Which resonates
Interweaving
Spirit
In physical form
From this you die
For this you are born.

The enigma of emerging from Earth

Always being of Her and yet more.